FOR

_____

This book is for you.

WITH LOVE

_____

ALSO BY REBECCA RAY

The Universe Listens to Brave

*Be Happy: 35 Powerful Methods for
Personal Growth & Well-Being*

The
ART *of*
Self-Kindness

REBECCA RAY

MACMILLAN

To my readers,
thank you for being on this path
of discovery and growth with me.
Please go gently with yourself.
All ways and always.

CONTENTS

THIS BOOK IS FOR ...

You, the one with sensitivity as a super-power
though you're still learning to offer it to yourself,

You, the first to share a kind word with others
even when your self-talk is rarely gentle,

You, known for your generosity
but who forgets to give to yourself,

You, who forgives easily, but not when you
look in the mirror, because you hold yourself
to a standard of goodness that's honourable,
but without the balance of permission
to make mistakes,

You, the one who needs a reminder of your
humanness and the importance of holding your
own heart as warmly as you hold others,

You, the one who questions your worthiness,
even though you're loved – so loved – but not
sure how to love yourself,

You, brave and willing, and you're here,
on a journey back to yourself
through the art of self-kindness.

DEAR READER

I'm thankful you're here: seeking to bring kindness to yourself, finding a softer way forward, following your dreams without fear of judgement from others, and especially without fear of judgement from yourself.
The art of self-kindness is exactly that: an art. There are no bullet-point lists or assembly instructions for something so fundamental to our wellbeing. Self-kindness is always more flow than force; less prescription and more progress.

In other words, I'm not here to tell you what to do to love yourself. But I am here to bring light to the possibilities of a life where you can consider yourself a friend.

This book is for you if you've ever found yourself participating in the destruction of your own spirit. It's for you if you've been told that you are your own worst critic. It's for you if you've ever wondered if there is a way to live without the constant threat of disapproval from within. This book is also for you if you are on your way to changing the disparaging inner voice – trying on the art of self-kindness, liking the way it feels, and wondering how else you might explore it.

These pages in your hands are an invitation to consider your relationship with yourself. You are the only one on earth who knows the complete and unadulterated truth about how you treat yourself. This book invites you to build the foundations of a relationship with yourself that nurtures, rather than depletes, you. It is my offering of small, papery reminders of the fragility of our deepest selves and what it means to bring love, respect and honouring to yourself, just as you would a friend.

Perhaps you'll open to a random page as a starting point to set your intention for self-kindness each day. Perhaps you'll choose the chapters currently defining your struggle as a guide to explore further within yourself. Perhaps you have been given this book by someone who wants you to see yourself in the light of goodness and love through which they already see you.

This book is not a shortcut to becoming your own best friend. As much as I wish it was that easy, I'm not a fan of Band-Aids or empty promises. As with any relationship in your life, your relationship with yourself is one that needs regular, mindful tending – the type that takes time and effort from now until your last breath. And it's this effort that's transformative: when you begin to recognise yourself as enough, you free yourself from the war within. Your potential expands infinitely, and your inner peace becomes accessible.

So, let's do the work together. We'll go gently into awareness and acceptance and create your unique art of self-kindness. And as we do, your life will change and your heart will love you for it.

Rebecca xo

Introduction

AND WE GO GENTLY

*I*t was a Thursday when I asked. I don't remember the weather, or the headlines, or if my dog and I walked that morning. I do remember, though, that I already knew the answer, and had probably known it for half a decade. But people who don't listen to themselves with respectful, kind ears tend to ignore the messages their deepest selves are trying to communicate (even if those messages have been trying to gain attention in one way or another for years). No, people who listen to themselves through filters of perfection and expectation and rigid obligation hear different versions of only one thing: you're not enough.

I wish that this kind of damaging internal dialogue could only continue for so long before an automatic kill switch is activated to silence the vilification. And maybe some people have such a switch. But in my case, after decades of listening, I can't say that this day was in any way automatic or self-limiting. Instead, it was desperate permission-seeking in the face of long-term self-implosion.

One of the perks of being a psychologist is that my friendship circle includes other therapists. One of the drawbacks of being a psychologist is that friends don't offer friends therapy, because our board of ethics

'People who don't listen to themselves with respectful, kind ears tend to ignore the messages their deepest selves are trying to communicate.'

doesn't love that sort of boundary entanglement (and rightly so). But we are each in the business of professional listening, a skill that becomes so instinctive that you take it with you between life roles, and it was with an empathic ear that my friend John received me as I quietly crumbled in the café that afternoon.

I was asking him because it was January. If December is the month of endings, January is the month of beginnings, and I couldn't bring myself to start another year that would inevitably be a repeat of the year before, or the five before that. It's not that I didn't have a good life. I did – outwardly. But inwardly, the self-destruction was at breaking point. I was working myself into the ground while pummelling myself for not being more than I was. I saw myself as inherently lacking – in what, specifically, I'm not sure. It was just a *feeling*, and one that was so uncomfortable that I had perfected a puppet-like dance of working harder, earning more, acquiring more hobbies, wearing nicer clothes, exercising more often and donning more masks over my authentic self, all in the hope that my audience (me) would finally clap and give me a break.

But I was a tough crowd, and burnout is often misinterpreted as 'Do more!' by the one being burned.

It was just after we ordered when I asked.

'What will happen if I stop?'

(Puppets don't do well when they are released from their ties. All I had known until now was the invisible strings of expectation and perceived judgement holding me up.)

'Nothing will happen, Beck. Your clients will see other helpers and life will go on. Your options are to continue pushing yourself beyond what's healthy and acceptable, or to start being kind to yourself. Your choice.'

I already knew this, but coming from the mouth of a friend, mentor and fellow professional, it sounded louder, the words surer of themselves than if they made a guest appearance in my head.

John continued. 'Nothing will change while you keep doing the same thing you've always done.'

'But what will I *do*?' (said in quiet hysterics and translated as 'I can't possibly stop this performance, can I?').

'Sometimes we need to create an empty space before we can create what will fill it.'

Please know I never take for granted how wise my friends are. This sentence rolled out of John's mouth into the space between us as casually as if he was asking me if I'd gotten around to washing my car yet (the answer to car-washing is always no). It's been inscribed on the walls of my mind since and the hope it offered was my life raft.

Neural pathways are wired through habit, and the habit of seeking worthiness outside myself in the form of *more* was so ingrained that I had misinterpreted the signs of burnout as a kind of fallibility I needed to master. We do what we've always done even when it's not working, unless we consciously stop the cycle. Unless we consciously choose something different for ourselves and then practise it repeatedly to strengthen those neural pathways. Habits of thinking are the most automatic (and therefore, most resistant to change) and it's in the shadows of our minds where the most destruction takes place. It's the hardest place to shine a light but, once we do, change is possible.

Here's the thing: the kindest people are often the hardest on themselves. They save their reserve tank of softness and compassion for others, even though their own was emptied long ago. There comes a point after which all our giving tanks are vulnerable to exhaustion. Mine were dry and rusting, which is not great considering my line of work required a considerable degree of giving. A human that doesn't give to themselves will eventually have nothing left for anyone else.

John's response to my pain was both to give me permission to give myself a break and a kick in the

'We do what we've always done even when it's not working, unless we consciously stop the cycle.'

19

backside for letting myself get to this point. Two weeks later, my practice was closed, my clients were referred on to trusted colleagues and my website was deactivated. My schedule was empty, and the future was blank. Oh, how I loathe blankness. Despite the urge to plan out some kind of future, I knew I had to sit in this space until I could move forward of my own volition – minus the dance designed to garner applause and confirm my worthiness. It was here that I learned to go gently.

It took a year of therapy and a few tantrums on my behalf. Turns out I was pretty attached to my own resistance, until somewhere along the way I realised that I was the one making my life abrasive. I was the one making things hard and jagged and unforgiving and cruel, and outwardly stopping was only a prefix to solving the problem. For the solution to be lifelong, I needed to start again differently: softly, kindly, with unconditional acceptance.

And that's where I remain, and where I'd like you to join me on the path – at the intersection of friendship to ourselves, where we move forward, kindly and gently.

Self-Acceptance

DEEP ROOTS, STEADY GROWTH

*I*met Jane when I was moonlighting as an assistant to my brother (it's a long story, best summarised as follows: his business needed extra hands and my wallet needed extra coins while I was on a break from clinical work). Jane's the kind of person who achieves more in a year than most of us would do in five. But, as we perfectionists tend to do, Jane sought within her accomplishments some kind of peace from the war of non-acceptance within herself.

We'd been working together for a month or so when Jane confessed that she had been struggling with anxiety for some time, phrased as an apology of sorts, as if she was disclosing an embarrassing flaw that she couldn't fix. Bravely, she committed to seeing a therapist. At the same time (and misguidedly), she also committed to metaphorically and literally chiselling her way into self-acceptance by training for a body-building competition.

For the next six months, I watched Jane continue trying to compensate for all the parts of herself that she saw as imperfect, broken and, ultimately, unacceptable. I watched her superhuman efforts: the 50-hour work week sandwiched between hours-long training sessions, meal preparation, macro counting and food weighing, while fulfilling her roles as wife, friend, daughter and sister in-between.

As Jane's weight dropped and her muscles strengthened, a paradox occurred: despite her Instagram-worthy body, the conditions around her self-acceptance became ever more stringent. Self-acceptance had become a mathematical equation. Had she added enough protein to her macro count? Would her body respond to the hours of cardio multiplied by weight training? Had the scale offered a subtraction that morning?

Bit by bit, Jane shrank – physically, emotionally and spiritually. Her relationship with herself disintegrated further and her anxiety spiralled out of control. The more we reject the parts of ourselves that don't fit with our expectations or unrelenting standards, the more we end up in pieces.

In pursuit of only the pleasant, pretty and pure shades of ourselves, wholeness is impossible. Fragmented affirmation of the self is the antithesis of self-acceptance because self-acceptance is an honouring of the entirety of the human condition. When we accept our strengths and our shortcomings, our joy and our suffering, we enter a deep understanding that wholeness is both light and shade. Images are one-dimensional without shadows – so it is with our humanness.

'The more we reject the parts of ourselves that don't fit with our expectations or unrelenting standards, the more we end up in pieces.'

Think of self-acceptance as the most robust of buttress roots. Buttress roots extend out from the base of a tree trunk from all sides in a series of wide tentacles that prop up the tree as it grows. These roots are not only wide, but long, maximising the ground cover from which they draw nutrients to give the tree its nourishment. Self-acceptance does exactly the same job when it comes to our wellbeing. It props us up, allowing us to grow taller and reach our full potential, while nourishing us as deeply as possible against the inevitable challenges and deficiencies in the environment around (and within) us. It's what keeps you standing when you fail, supports you when you're faced with your imperfections and sustains you as you evolve to your highest self.

Without the scaffolding of self-acceptance, the conditions we place on ourselves are unstable and leave us vulnerable to collapse under their unachievable weight. And it was in the collapse that Jane saw herself properly for the first time. For her, the beauty in the breakdown was in the choice it offered. She had the choice to continue discriminating against her imperfections, or to reassemble herself with mindful attention to every part being sacred and whole. If I introduced you to Jane today, you'd see what she chose in the relaxation of her shoulders and the softness of her eyes. Acceptance is her way now, and there's not a calculator in sight.

SELF-KINDNESS RITUAL

To cultivate acceptance, try ...

A VOW OF SELF-ACCEPTANCE

Make a vow of self-acceptance with the following offering.
Keep these words somewhere you can read them often, and
repeat them to yourself daily, or return to them when you
become disconnected from yourself.

To Myself,

I see you. I see how hard you try and how much you give.
I see your strengths and your imperfections, your wisdom
and your learnings. I see the parts of you that are scared
and the parts of you that are brave. I see the parts of you
that are healed and the parts that are still healing. I see
you practising and growing. I see it all, and I accept it all,
without conditions, expectations or judgement. I accept
every part of you exactly as you are in this moment.
You are entirely enough.

Love,

Myself xo

She realised her power
only when

she came to accept
and love herself just
as she was.

The power from that
space is infinite.

True self-acceptance shows up
in that moment when you realise
that peace cannot co-exist with war.
It shows up in the moment
you choose to
stop being your own enemy
and to love yourself instead.

There were pieces of her history

she didn't quite have a place for yet.

But that's okay,

because making sense of experience
takes time.

We need to expand.

Open up.

Come to understanding.

And then we can see all along that

even while we are figuring it out,
we are still whole.

May the past be
your teacher,
not your captor.

She found a place within
that's soft and forgiving
and respectful and brave.
She lives there now.

Our relationship with ourselves

shapes our entire life.

Make sure it's reflective

of the relationship you'd like to

have with someone who is with

you on a permanent basis.

You know the friend that
you are to others?

You can be that friend
to yourself, too.

When it's all said and done

I want to be able to say I loved.

I loved fiercely the hearts

that captured mine.

I loved life for its gift of being.

I loved myself without conditions

or judgement.

Peace is not the place where
our inner world is perfectly calm.

Peace is the place where
we accept that

there are parts of us
that will always be
in conflict and contradiction.

This is both our wholeness
and humanness.

The process of allowing ourselves
to be human means allowing the
times we choose to:

give up,

ignore advice,

ignore ourselves,

shut down,

or run away.

This is us at our most vulnerable.

This is when we need to accept ourselves
(and each other) most.

Self-Truth

THE MIRROR ASKS ONLY TO SEE YOU

*I*t's a tough gig being an outsider. I'm the introvert on the outskirts of an extroverted world. I'm the sensitive one with big feelings, looked upon with curiosity by a family who prefer to keep emotions compact and out of the way. Mine is the stretch-marked, lumpy post-baby body that's soft, wrinkled and large in the places our culture says should be hard, smooth and small. I'm in love with a woman without identifying as a lesbian. Boxes aren't comfortable, but I'd be lying if I didn't tell you that until I was into my thirties I tried to contort myself into a shape that allowed me to fit in as many boxes as possible. This was until I worked out that the psychological and practical gymnastics needed to mould myself into what I perceived to be acceptable is bloody exhausting, not to mention ineffective. The closer I came to fitting in, the further away I was from my true self.

Is this you, too? Trying to fit into boxes that weren't designed for you, but ignoring the discomfort and forcing yourself into them anyway? It's okay to say 'yes'. You're safe in embracing your humanness here. And if we humans are conspicuous in anything, it's altering ourselves for the purpose of belonging.

But when we deviate too far from our true selves, even if it's in the service of belonging, it's dangerous for our sense of self. We risk reaching a place where we are no longer sure of our own identity. We risk taking on a persona whose purpose is to please someone else – a playdough version of ourselves

'The closer I came to fitting in, the further away I was from my true self.'

that's designed to yield to the prodding of the strongest outside force, whether that be society, our parents, our partner, or the idea that we have about ourselves that we believe to be more palatable. The question is, who are you bending for? Who are you turning yourself inside-out for? Who are you seeking approval from?

It's true our culture doesn't help. The pressure we put on each other is both conscious and unconscious. We are imbued with beliefs that we must be more, have more and do more, while weighing less, making it look effortless and being fearless. It's a social house of mirrors, each pane of glass reflecting the requisites we place on each other – the judgement, expectation, calls for perfection, demands for agreeable opinions and ways of being that are comfortable for everyone else to exist beside. What society reflects back upon us is simply an expression of where a culture is at emotionally and socially. But sometimes we forget that the manicured feeds scrolling under our thumbs through which we see that expression are dangerously believable.

It's risky to be authentic. It's rebellious to be different. Rejection is a real and painful possibility that no one willingly signs up for. It's far more comfortable to avoid the risk and move further away from ourselves, into identities that are not ours, into highlight reels and smiles of concealment, into saying yes when we'd really like to say no, and into continuing to do things we think we should do over things we'd prefer to be doing.

Consider where you might have done this in your own life. Which parts of yourself have been altered or hidden because you were frightened of the reaction if they were to be seen?

I wonder what your experience would be if you removed the mask and allowed yourself to stand in front of a mirror that asks nothing more than to see the real you. The thing is, lovely one, the world will only ever respond to you as you show up. You have the choice to show up in disguise, but I promise you that the energy of fabricating your identity will be wearying, and you'll eventually tire of doubting whether you are loved for the real you or the contrived you. The ones who stand tallest are the ones who show up in their own shoes and leave unique footprints. Isn't it time you walked your own path through the world?

SELF-KINDNESS RITUAL

_____

TRUTH-SEEKER EXERCISE

Write down where you are not being true to yourself in the
following life areas. Be as specific as possible. This exercise
is not about promoting self-criticism. It's about bringing your
true self out of the shadows and acknowledging where you've
been hiding or offering up a false version of yourself. Notice
how it feels to acknowledge the parts of you that you've been
ignoring or dismissing or covering over. Notice how it feels to
give yourself permission to be truly seen. Consider what life
would be like if you were to step out of the shadows and into
the light with your full self. Courage trumps fear every time!

RELATIONSHIPS: _____

_____

WORK: _____

_____

PARENTING: _____

_____

PERSONAL GROWTH: _____

_____

HEALTH: _____

_____

HOBBIES/INTERESTS: _____

_____

She learned to stop walking
on the outskirts of her life,

too scared to dip her toes into
the waters of full existence,

too scared of judgement,

too scared to be her true Self.

And when she finally dived in,
she wished she'd found
such freedom sooner.

We find 'our people'

when we start

being ourselves.

Authenticity is not the
path of the masses.

It takes courage to stand
in your own skin
and be exactly as you are:

imperfectly beautiful
and one of a kind.

Will you honour yourself
to do just that?

Integrity sometimes
demands that we get
uncomfortable if
we choose to stand
by our values.

But short-term pain
is always preferable
to long-term destruction
of our spirit.

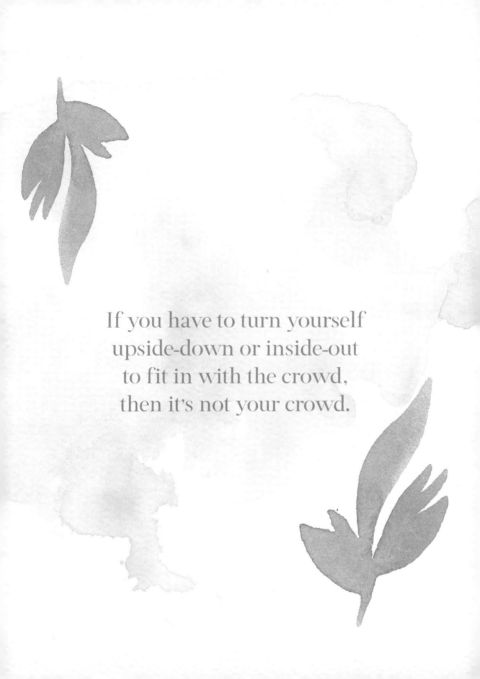

If you have to turn yourself
upside-down or inside-out
to fit in with the crowd,
then it's not your crowd.

You can tell she knows herself

because there's conviction in the way she says 'No',

and possibility in the way she says 'Yes'.

Don't ever apologise
for your growth.

No one has to understand
your journey but you.

She refused to dilute
her spirit

to fit someone else's
expectations.

She wasn't in the habit
of betraying her
authentic Self.

She once wore the expectations
of others heavily,

an invisibility cloak that kept
her from seeing herself.

But she awoke, opened her eyes
and saw that her authenticity

was too beautiful to hide.
And she stepped into the light.

Never apologise for creating your life around what you know about yourself.

Your people will understand.

Many won't.

But your greatest gift to yourself and the world is authenticity.

Self-Talk

THE VOICE OF A FRIEND

I wanted to begin this chapter with an example of the impact of negative self-talk. I was running through the library of memories in my mind for a story to jump out at me, one that perfectly articulated toxic internal chatter. I realised that I don't have just one story I could tell because there's not a person I've known personally or professionally who hasn't come undone at some stage thanks to hurtful internal dialogue.

There's the friend of mine who has started three businesses in the space of 12 months and followed none of them through because her mind tells her she will fail. And the elite athlete I know who is stripped of confidence as a result of his mind telling him that professional athletes are laughing at his on-the-side sporting endeavours and not taking him seriously. There's my wife, who almost convinced herself that she had no talent after she failed to get through the blind auditions on *The Voice*. And there's almost every client I've ever treated who has sat opposite me asking for help for the pain they experience in response to self-talk that is critical, limiting and damaging.

Self-talk is a conversation between you and yourself that occurs largely outside of your awareness. It's this unmonitored voice(s) that wields the most power over our mood, especially when it's judging, labelling, condemning and otherwise shrinking us. Imagine if there was a person who

'Destructive self-talk is
the invisible obstacle
that trips you up
whenever you attempt
to step forward.'

followed you around every minute of the
day providing a running commentary about
you that was undermining, unsupportive,
damning and downright mean. Self-talk is
this kind of shadow for many of us. And if you talk to yourself
in this way, what does this mean for your confidence and
motivation? Your self-worth and sense of agency in the world?
For reaching your potential or recovering from failure or
rejection? Destructive self-talk is the invisible obstacle that
trips you up whenever you attempt to step forward.

Sometimes, we get a break. When we are in a state of flow
and deeply engaged in an activity, the conversation tends to
quieten, or at least be focused on the activity at hand; and
in times of joy or contentment the chatter usually becomes
lighter. But these times are the exception, and for those of us
who tend toward worrier-mode over warrior-mode, the radio
playing in the background is mostly negative.

I promise I'm not going to spout pop psychology and
suggest that you just 'think positive'. This would ignore the
fact we have evolved to take our minds very seriously, given
their job is to warn us of threats. Once upon an ancestral
time, having a mind that warned of rival clans encroaching
upon our territory and prompted us to search for food and
water sources was a necessity in the daily task of staying alive.

Unfortunately, the software in the fear centre of our brains is yet to catch up with the fact that we are quite successful at surviving nowadays. Instead of relaxing a little, our minds still worry, and we still automatically listen, taking on a 24/7 broadcast with a tendency to be a tad more melodramatic than our lived reality.

You don't have the luxury of buying into everything that your mind says if you're out to live an inspired, expansive life. I'm not implying that you like having an inner critic who's a little too fond of their own voice. All I'm saying is that what's automatic doesn't require effort. Being mindless is effortless. And what it gets you is more criticism. More personal attacks. More paralysis. Bringing awareness to your self-talk is hard. It requires conscious effort, willingness and consistent practise, and conscious habit change – especially for cognitive processes – is always easier said than done. But you'll never get a different result without actively participating in a different (mindful) approach.

Brain software that has evolved over millennia doesn't change overnight. But you can know the freedom of disengaging from your self-talk by becoming aware of it and speaking to yourself as you would a friend. Awareness is where you'll find your peace, and peace is a daily practice in tiny acts of self-kindness like mindful self-talk.

SELF-KINDNESS RITUAL

THE FRIENDLY/FRIEND'S RESPONSE

The following steps will help you bring mindful awareness to your internal conversation, to help you shift from self-talk that blocks you to self-talk that supports and encourages you.

1. Bring awareness to your thoughts. We can't respond differently when we are being mindless. Step back and observe what your mind is saying.

2. Consider what your closest friend would say in response to any criticism, condemnation or negativity that your mind is giving you.

3. Respond silently in your mind (or out loud if you feel comfortable doing so), in a tone that is gentle and understanding. Respond as if you were your own friend: supportive, loving, but also not willing to allow you to cop out or go down a path that's not helpful.

4. Practise daily, as much as possible. The more you practise this skill, the more it will become your default response style.

Please lay down
your weapons

in your relationship
with yourself.

When the war is
no longer,

we make way for
peace to come.

The mind is very
good at its job.

Be careful that you
are not seduced by
your own excuses.

You'll find lightness
when you drop
the weight

of what you think
other people are thinking
about you.

Hold your
thoughts lightly.

The looser your grip,

the more easily
you can let go

of thoughts that
aren't helping

you go where you
want to go.

The words you
say to yourself

are the roots of
your growth.

Let them nourish
and strengthen you,

not drain and
damage you.

Perhaps those
gentle words

that you offer others
are the same words that

would soothe your
heart right now

if you were to give
them to yourself.

The words you say to yourself

act as scaffolding around
your sense of worthiness.

Every kind and gentle word
protects your worthiness.

Every criticism and invalidation
tears it down.

Assemble thoughtfully.

If we're going to get real about
being gentle with ourselves,

then we need to start
underneath our skin.

We need to start with the
words we say to ourselves

and the compassion we
offer to our own pain.

That's where the change lives.

The war stops

when we stop speaking
to ourselves

with weapons disguised
as words.

You can't possibly rise

if you're still running
a story in your head

about how you should
have predicted
the fall.

Self-Compassion

HOLD YOUR HURT
WITH GENTLE HANDS

*T*here are things you've experienced that have scarred you. Things that have changed the trajectory of your life because of the pain they've caused. There is hurt that sits in the recesses of your heart. It doesn't make a noise, but its weight can't be ignored. These are the wounds that you try not to think about or can't stop thinking about. This is the pain that you try not to talk about or can't stop talking about.

We all carry it – a kind of unspeakable or unshakeable pain from the waypoints in life that have demanded to be seen and remembered. As unique as the map of veins underneath your skin, their blue-red pulsing is as individual as the stories that created it.

We can't avoid it. Life hurts.

You'd be forgiven for wishing to turn your sensitivity off, or for wanting immunity from all that's harsh in the world. But I'm here to ask you not to fold into yourself. Your sensitivity is how you receive the full experience of living in all its beauty, bravery and barbarity. You are not alone in hurting, but turning off your capacity to feel will rob you of richness and colour.

I see how far you've come despite the pain you carry. However, for the times the wounds are cumbersome, and hold you back in some way, I want to talk about not what you're carrying, but *how* you carry it. You see, it's our relationship with suffering that defines its place as either a wall or a doorway in our lives. It can limit you or it can transform you, depending on what you do with it. If you dismiss your suffering, or drown in it, if you criticise it or approach it with contempt, then expect to also be driven to shut down, turn away from yourself and harden yourself against the world. The difficulty with this hardening process is that although it feels protective, it closes you off from the healing and growth and beauty to come. Each hurt becomes another wall to climb or stay behind.

There is another way.

It's possible to soften towards yourself, towards your suffering, and to hold your pain gently. Compassion is the gift you can offer yourself as an invitation to personal growth and healing. It doesn't take away the pain, but it will change your experience of it. Think of it as cushioning in your relationship with yourself. It sits around your heart as insulation from all that's abrasive in life, showing up as acknowledgement and understanding for your experiences. Self-compassion is the state of holding our own pain respectfully, kindly and with empathy, just as you would for a friend. 'This is hard. I see you're in pain. You are not alone.' The opposite of self-compassion is apathy – to cast your own feelings aside as unimportant and not worthy of being seen through kind eyes.

It's true that self-compassion gets a bad rap. It's easily misinterpreted as selfish and indulgent. But it's not permission to wallow, ignore others or avoid responsibilities. It's not a leave pass from life. It's not a dispensation to back away from, go around or otherwise avoid the hard things we face. Self-compassion is not a victim state. It's the place where we join with ourselves, gently giving our pain room before we recover and rise.

My invitation to you is to offer yourself compassion for every part of your suffering: from critical thoughts about yourself, to mistakes you've refused to forgive, to stories you continue to run in your head about how you would have, should have or could have. Bring gentleness to the habits that aren't working for you, the places you feel stuck and to the changes you seek but haven't yet actioned. Feel what it's like to bring compassion to yourself. Feel what it's like to hold yourself in a place where you hurt rather than condemn yourself or make yourself defective or wrong for having pain. This is how to honour your humanity. This is how you befriend yourself.

ONCE UPON A TIME

Imagine hearing your life story for the first time, with a special focus on the painful events you've experienced that have left scars that continue to need tending. Imagine you are sitting opposite yourself, telling your listening self about everything you've been through: the pain you've seen, felt and heard, the parts of you that are struggling to forgive, and the parts you wish had never happened but continue to try and accept.

Listen with compassionate ears. Hold your pain gently. Remember that this is not something you're watching on Netflix. This is real life and you've lived it, felt it and had (or are finding) the courage to work through it. Acknowledge yourself for this. See your pain through the eyes of empathy and see how it feels to approach yourself compassionately.

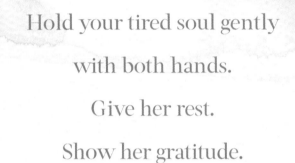

Hold your tired soul gently

with both hands.

Give her rest.

Show her gratitude.

Remind her there's magic

of which she can't yet know

in the days to come.

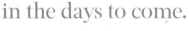

Sometimes taking
a step backwards
is the gift you need
to learn a lesson
completely.

I'm just going to hold it all gently.

The uncertainty.

The hope.

The mistakes.

The calling.

The past.

The story of not good enough.

The impatience to heal.

All of it.

I'm just going to hold it gently.

She may not have arrived
here quickly.

But in every softening edge
and compassionate word,

every forgiving nod
and encouraging push,

in every gentle practice she
gifted herself,

she found
the art of self-kindness.

Treat your past
with gentle hands.

It's given you the
lessons you needed

to be where
you are now.

She learned to listen
to what she needs.

To rest.

To carry on.

To be patient.

To be persistent.

To believe in her dreams.

After all, self-respect
starts with listening
to her own Self.

A little reminder for those who
hold another's pain gently,
but forget their own;

reach out to another
in their time of need,
but don't reach out to themselves;

use up their caring outside
before remembering to
offer it within . . .

Please,

love + love yourself.

Love + love yourself.

Love + love yourself.

Sometimes the
kindest thing you can
do for yourself

is just take a minute
to process it all.

Take that kind heart
of yours and
offer it as much to
yourself as you
do to others.

Hold your hurt
with gentle hands.

Acknowledge it
for what it is.

Give it room.

Like people, pain
softens when it's seen
and accepted.

Self-Worth

WORTHINESS CANNOT
BE MEASURED

*A*t this point, I'd like to invite you to stop and take a breath. Inhale deeply. Exhale completely. I want to remind you that I'm beside you as you take these pages into your heart and into your life. The art of self-kindness is beautiful, but rarely does it come naturally. I believe all the chapters in this book are uniquely important for our practice of self-kindness, but it's self-worth that I'd consider to be the canvas upon which everything else is painted. Without a canvas, there's no foundation. Without self-worth, every other aspect of self-kindness is colourless.

If I'm honest though, I wish this chapter was unnecessary. I wish that a deep knowing of our sense of worthiness was innate for each of us. Unfortunately, the assumption of worth is usually fractured at some point in childhood, marking the beginning of our efforts to tie our value to conditions and standards of which we're barely yet aware. By the time we're adults, stable self-worth requires that we unlearn to hold ourselves up to any number of (invalid) social, cultural, parental, institutional and self-imposed measuring sticks.

Because doing so only buys into the idea that you must be something other than what you are in order to be worthy.

Take my friend Jen, a gifted writer. She's a copywriter who dabbles in fiction on the side, having successfully turned her art into a career. But her success has come at an unexpected cost. Jen described herself as being a 'good girl' growing up. She enjoyed a close relationship with her mum and dad and, with their encouragement and guidance, finished school, went to university and joined the corporate world, with a few letters being added after her name upon earning her degree. She wasn't long in her new role before she realised that 9 to 5 life wasn't for her. She'd taken the *safe* road (i.e. the road her parents expected her to take), but this wasn't the road that led to her fulfilment. When she chose to quit her job and write professionally, Jen discovered her parents' attachment to the course they'd set for her was strong enough that they defined Jen's worthiness by her career choices. Anything other than this path was considered *less than* by her parents, who actively lobbied for her to return to her 'proper' job, and all but disowned her when she refused. Jen has had to do a significant amount of grief and healing work to come to a place where she can acknowledge herself as worthy even while pursuing a career that makes her parents uncomfortable.

Let's get clear on something: no one else gets to cast judgement on your choices and use that information to evaluate your worthiness. Not your parents, not your teachers, not society, not social media. No one.

If you give up your power in this way, the result can only be dissonance between the life you want to create for yourself and the life someone else tries to design for you. Soon enough, it will be you that's doubting your own worth because if you're measured enough by the outside world, measuring yourself becomes a habit.

I'm relieved to say that Jen continues to pursue the things that make her heart sing, even though her parents' non-acceptance hurts her. We don't have control over other people's attachment to their ideas of how the world should be. But we do have control over living by our values, and if there's one thing you can measure, it's how closely you are living by your values and taking action toward the things that you decide make your life meaningful and worthwhile.

At some point, we must take the responsibility for our self-worth away from the significant people in our lives and hold it squarely and firmly in our own hands. The beginnings of personal peace come when we are able to sustain our own self-worth. No one can give worthiness to you, just as no one can take it from you. Your worthiness just *is,* but your wisdom around its presence depends on cultivating the intuitive practice of reminding yourself that you are enough. My wish for you is that you know the contentment of waking up and loving yourself all over again.

SELF-KINDNESS RITUAL

REWRITE THE STORY OF
NOT ENOUGH

I want you to think about your story of 'not enough'.
The one that you've heard a million times, that's
probably been playing in your head since you were at
school, or since that defining event when you felt
ashamed or rejected or broken (or all of these). It plays
whenever you think of following your dreams, making
a significant change or getting out of your comfort zone.
And when it plays, it convinces you that you'll never
make it, you don't deserve it, you can't do it, you're
a failure, there's something wrong with you and
ultimately, you're not worthy.

And now I want you to rewrite it. For real. I want you
to write your story of 'enough', the new version that you'll
carry with you from now on that affirms your worthiness,
your value, your strengths, your power, your beauty and
your place in the world. This is a story of honouring. Give
it the time and space and respect it deserves and then keep
it somewhere you can re-read it whenever you need to.

And then, under the
breath of the moon,

she realised she
was enough.

Always was and
always will be.

You are worthy.

Full stop.

No conditions.

No fine print.

No timeframe.

No expectations.

No price.

Comparison is the most dangerous
territory for self-worth.

Be gentle enough with yourself
to forgive your imperfections today,

and respectful enough to aim
for growth tomorrow.

Self-respect is just as much
about saying no to situations
and people that don't nourish
you as it is about saying
yes to opportunities and
possibilities that stretch
your comfort zone.

The way you
catch yourself
in the fall
determines how
(and when)
you'll fly again.

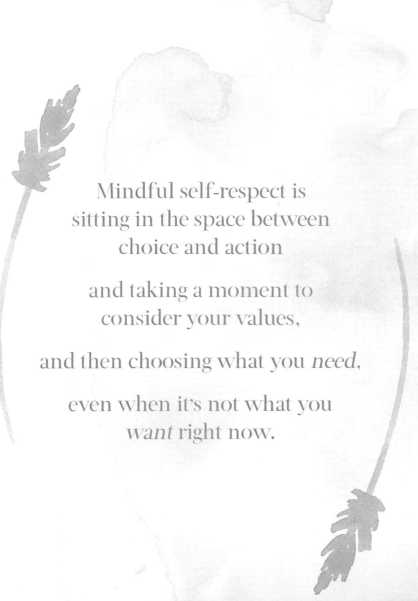

Mindful self-respect is
sitting in the space between
choice and action

and taking a moment to
consider your values,

and then choosing what you *need*,

even when it's not what you
want right now.

You are enough.

There is no reason to keep
testing and grading yourself
to see if you pass.

There is no competition for
worth or wholeness.

You only have to see this
to find peace.

There was a settling of
her soul as soon as she closed
the door on 'not enough'.

The funny thing was that she didn't
have to go looking for peace.

It arrived when she stopped
investing in beliefs

that voluntarily destroyed
her worth.

Things you don't need
permission for:

1. Saying no.

2. Following your dreams.

3. Choosing yourself.

And in the end,

of all the things I wish
to say about my life,

most importantly I want
to be able to say

I was doing life the
best I knew how,

and learning continuously
to do it better.

Self-Belief

THE INNER FAITH TO TRY

*I*t was a client who first introduced me to the idea of doing a vision board with photos hung on string with tiny little pegs. The vision boards I had known previously were always the traditional 'board' kind, until I saw Kate's and fell in love with the creativity and detail with which she'd embraced the exercise. But as she was showing me photos of her handiwork hanging on her living-room wall under fairy lights, she became tearful. This wasn't just a pretty exercise to her. It was a mirror that reflected back her deepest hopes and dreams. She was particularly affected by one goal that she was convinced was out of reach. She craved adventure and wanted to move overseas for 12 months. Because she struggled with anxiety, she'd come to believe she'd never be able to make it happen.

Kate captured the goal on her vision board hoping it would shake her awake, hoping it would challenge the fear into submission. But instead, the fear had grown, and she was already grieving in anticipation of failing – or worse, never trying in the first place. She'd bought into some of the most common myths that show up around following our dreams: that you can only start when you feel ready, you must be fearless and you must feel 100 per cent confident.

I called bullshit. I wasn't going to stand by and allow Kate to give away her ambitions for beliefs that are promoted as aspirational but are largely unachievable. Here's the thing: self-belief isn't what you think it is – at least, not the way I work with it. Self-belief is allowing yourself to try even with fear present, *and* independent of the outcome. The two co-exist. Fear is a warning system that you are entering unfamiliar territory that may hold some kind of threat. Self-belief is guidance and encouragement from your inner self to explore, to experiment, to go beyond what's comfortable in the service of living an expansive life. We need both.

Kate wanted to burst through the invisible walls of her comfort zone to do the most courageous thing she'd ever done. She was scared. She didn't think she'd ever be ready. She couldn't remember the last time she felt confident. I wasn't concerned about any of these feelings that she saw as barriers to her dreams. I was concerned about the fact that she wasn't giving herself permission to even *try*.

Know this: you don't need all your emotional ducks in a row before you have a go.

You'll know you struggle with self-belief because it shows up in some common disguises: procrastination; empty promises ('I'll do it when …'); seeking permission or approval from others; indecision; and making excuses for your inaction and then making excuses for your excuses.

Kate had done all of these. Imagine how well it would have gone down if I'd chosen to respond with a trite one-liner like 'Just believe you can, and you *will*!' I'm not into grandiose and potentially false promises, because what's true is there's a chance you *won't*. Failure is always a risk when we're out to do something bigger or more difficult than we've previously known.

Self-belief is more complex than feeling confident. It's a combination of saying *yes* to an experience, fuelled by hope and possibility, and the willingness to go forth with no guarantees and the courage to see it through even when it gets hard. It takes guts to give yourself the benefit of the doubt. Self-belief is not fearlessness, or supreme confidence, or perfect readiness, or the unshakeable belief in success. It's placing trust in yourself to give your all to the experience. It's the freedom from self-imposed limits before you've tested the waters.

With anxiety as a passenger on this, her bravest path, Kate booked her flights later that day. She realised she had faith in herself to try when she had the freedom to move through the experience imperfectly. Please give yourself permission for the goals you'd peg on your own vision strings. Self-belief is opening the door to possibility and taking fear with you on the ride.

SELF-KINDNESS RITUAL

MAGNIFICENCE REMINDER LIST

For the times you forget your own magnificence,
I want you to record it here and put this list somewhere
you'll see it every day. Too often we focus on our perceived
failings and weaknesses, placing them in a box of things
we must iron out, disentangle and make pretty.
It's rare that we focus on our strengths, but doing
so is a powerful boost on the way to self-belief.

_____

_____

_____

_____

_____

_____

VISION BOARD

Grab your string and your pegs, or your cardboard or
corkboard. Take your scissors and collate all the pictures
and words that represent the future you're out to create
for yourself. You could make it time-limited (e.g. pictures
representing the coming year), or simply images that
represent the life that's meaningful for you for the foreseeable
future. Place it somewhere you'll see it daily. May this
inspiration remind you why it's worth believing in yourself!

She's brave enough to care.

She's brave enough to stand
up for what she believes in.

She's brave enough to take action
that makes a difference in
this world.

Even when it's hard,
and some are trying to tear
her down, and she aches from
the effort of trying, she's brave
enough to keep going.

She stopped waiting for a guarantee.

She stopped waiting to feel ready.

She stopped waiting for
everyone's approval.

And she started creating
the space to try.

She started moving
forward anyway.

She started backing herself.
And that's when it all changed.

She whispered her
dreams to the stars,
as they blinked
knowingly down
upon her.

'I'm listening,' the
Universe replied.

Today is a good
day to stop and
remind yourself how
great you're doing.

She finally learned
that she could only
get as far as her
self-belief allowed.

Progress beckons those
who back themselves.

Heart: 'I believe in you!'

Mind: 'But here are all the reasons you shouldn't.'

Soul: 'Here's to the believers.'

Perhaps it's time to stop
and see that you're actually
doing it – this living thing.

You are putting one foot
in front of the other
and doing the best
you can.

And that's all you need
to do right now.

You might not recognise her now.

She's changed, but not in a way
that's different from herself.

In a way that's closer to who
she is than she's ever been.

That's what happens when
you start believing in yourself –
you meet yourself anew.

It's not about how many
times you need to let go.

Or how many times
you need to heal.

Or how many times
you need to start again.

It's about the fact
that you did,
and you can,
and you will.

She stopped
thinking about it
and started doing it.

And that was just
the beginning.

Self-Forgiveness

FORGIVENESS IS A
LIFE-PRESERVER

I wonder what the concept of self-forgiveness makes you feel? Is it relieving? Perhaps it gives you the sense that you could stop holding your breath and exhale fully. Or maybe it's sharp – something that's too overwhelming to consider when it comes to yourself? I'm not under any illusion that this topic is light, especially because it likely triggers your mind to offer you a selection of your most painful memories. But I'm here to ask you to stay with me as we explore it, because self-forgiveness is a life-preserver. Without it, I've seen people fade away under the darkness of a life lived in the captivity of regret. I don't want that for you.

Forgiveness is not just an outward expression we offer others. It's an essential characteristic of a healthy relationship with ourselves. Self-forgiveness is an acknowledgement of the stumbling nature of the human condition, with our own imperfections, personal evolution and inevitable mistakes. It's no small thing. That doesn't mean it's impossible, it simply means it's necessary.

Because punishment isn't the way of self-kindness.

Withholding forgiveness from yourself when faced with your mistakes keeps you captive to the past. It chains you to a time and place that hurt you (and maybe hurt someone else, too), but in trapping you there, it only presses on the bruise with no capacity for atonement or healing.

Before you have a chance to become incensed at this gentle approach to things you perhaps believe you should be castigated for, let me clarify that self-forgiveness is not a get-out-of-jail-free card. Its purpose is not to minimise the gravity of the situation or your remorse for your actions. There is a time and place for reflection on mistakes and leaning into the learning experience. Apologies and amends are necessary and deserve an appropriate amount of energy. But to permanently punish yourself only keeps you in the mistake. Self-forgiveness is the way out of self-loathing, haunting guilt and shame, and paralysing self-condemnation. It stops you from being forever sentenced to walking on the outskirts of life in the blind hope that doing so minimises any future mistakes you might make. It allows you to live into a braver future, with space to be vulnerable, imperfect, always learning and willing to try despite the risk of not getting it right.

There are no shortcuts though. Conditional forgiveness won't fly as a substitute for wholehearted, all-encompassing self-forgiveness. Forgiving yourself means forgiving all of it, not just the pieces that are more acceptable than the rest. It's not true self-forgiveness if it's attached to a condition that's outside of your control ('I forgive myself as long as X forgives me, too') or persecutes you indefinitely ('I forgive myself as long as I never make a mistake again'). And it's not true self-forgiveness if you don't follow through by speaking kindly to yourself, making room for your healing process and ultimately, giving yourself another chance.

You can see why I'm always reminding you to go gently, can't you? There are so many corners to these self-kindness processes where we can easily fall back into self-critical and harsh mistreatment of ourselves. I promise that your efforts will be worth it – not just for you, but for the people you love, too. When we are more forgiving to ourselves, we are more forgiving to others. Our relationships become deeper, braver and more open-hearted.

I don't know what your mistakes have been. I don't know what you regret. But I do know that if you don't give yourself another chance, how on earth do you shift? You can't know what you don't know before you know it. The quality of your relationship with yourself depends on your capacity to embrace your humanness. We can't always come to self-forgiveness alone though. Sometimes a therapist, mentor, spiritual advisor or trusted friend can be the balm between us and our mistakes, offering a different perspective and a compassionate ear. However you find your way to forgiveness, simply know there's nothing more powerful you can offer yourself when it comes to living freely, fully and courageously. Please give yourself the gift of freedom, repeatedly, as many times as it takes.

FORGIVENESS FOR
YOUR YOUNGER SELF

Write a letter to your younger self – when you
were 15 or 21 or 36, or perhaps simply
yesterday's version of you.

Acknowledge where or how you violated your own
values. Reflect on how you came to take the actions
you took. Have compassion for where you were at,
at the time. Have compassion for your motivations.
Have compassion for what you thought you knew to
be true at the time. Reflect on how you did or didn't
made amends. These reflections bring empathy to
the wisdom you're gathering from your mistakes.
Remind yourself that it's only through the painful
lessons that we evolve into wiser, kinder, more
willing versions of ourselves.

It hurt. And she carried on.

It failed. And she carried on.

It broke. And she carried on.

She carried on. And it passed.

She carried on. And it changed.

She carried on. And it was beautiful.

You know that
time you were
broken and hurting,
but then you showed
up and gave yourself
another chance?

That was beautiful.

Do that again.

Sometimes the bravest thing you can do is offer forgiveness to yourself.

You can't move forward while you're still wasting energy on yesterday's mistakes.

She chose to forgive herself.

She chose to befriend herself.

She chose to soften
towards herself.

Because continuing
to do otherwise was
to participate in the
destruction of her spirit.

And that's not her
way anymore.

Choices you can make:

1. To forgive instead of condemn yourself.

2. To be your own ally instead of enemy.

3. To stay instead of walk out on yourself.

Accept the new beginning
offered in your next breath.
In your waking tomorrow.
In your choice to forgive
where you could've done better.
You're allowed to start again
whenever you need to.

She learned that forgiveness
is a practice.

That sometimes we must forgive
ourselves for not forgiving.

Sometimes we walk in parallel
with it for a while,

before we let it take our hand.

That's okay, because she's
still here, practising.

Perhaps it's time to stop
being so hard on your heart.

Can't you see she's doing the
best she can to stay standing
against all that's cold and harsh
and hurtful in the world?

Forgive her for beating so fast.

She's just trying to keep up.

Hold her gently.

Remind her to exhale.

Let her rest today.

Forgive the parts of you that
didn't know better at the time.

Forgive the parts of you that
could've done better at the time.

Forgive the parts of you that care so
much they have paralysed you from
moving forward until it's 'fixed'.

Forgiveness is release.
It's only through releasing
yourself that you can heal
and do better next time.

Today's choice:

To reject any story
you're running in your
head that damages
your spirit.

Self-Trust

SHOW UP FOR YOURSELF

*T*here is nothing quite so disconcerting as the sense of abandonment that comes from not being able to trust yourself. It won't always look the same, but it will always feel the same: a deep-seated uneasiness that kicks in when you've headed off in a direction that's no longer consistent with what matters to you deep down. I'm talking about the times when you've:

- needed to have your own back but, for whatever reason, haven't;
- lied to yourself about how you're doing;
- quit before you've given yourself a chance to start;
- been the most critical voice you're listening to;
- refused help or not asked for it;
- run when you needed to stay;
- stayed when you needed to go;
- believed and acted as though you're not (and perhaps never will be) enough.

It's a form of betrayal, this walking away from oneself. It's an insidious and quiet mistrust against your mind, heart and soul. I know this because I've done it. I've tiptoed, walked and flat-stick run out on myself. I've done it when the stakes weren't that high, like with the gym membership I purchased and used for a month but paid for a year. And I've done it when the stakes were so high that I suffered deeply for years afterwards. That story is bigger than I have words for here but suffice to say I hit 10 on the self-abandonment scale, where 0 is 'present and accounted for' and 10 is 'looks like she's never coming back'. This was before I learned the art of treating myself kindly, back when I talked about self-love as a noun rather than a verb – it's far easier to convince yourself you have self-love than to actually practise it.

I've come to believe that running out on ourselves is circular. Inevitably, we end up back in front of the mirror where we face the same choice: to show up for ourselves or to run again. To acknowledge the truth or continue deceiving ourselves. To do what we know we need or to continue to do only what's comfortable.

I don't need to tell you how many times we run before we show up. (Quite a few *winks*.)

Eventually, there comes a time when the parts of you that are brave will intuitively know that you can't keep running away from yourself if you want to live fully and richly. That wise voice deep in your gut will continue to whisper to you, asking you over and over to come back. And when you do, you'll be welcomed. You'll have to work through all the hard feelings and face all the hard truths, but that's the point where trusting yourself becomes something you are actively participating in.

Alignment is like that. It's not always comfortable, but at the same time, it's a coming home of sorts. A sense of coming back to yourself. I can't say exactly what showing up will look like for you, but here are my observations of the process. Self-trust is about:

- listening to your intuition while tuning out the white noise of others' expectations;
- peeling back the discomfort of your mistakes so that you can see the lessons;
- gathering your self-knowledge and doing what you know needs to be done;
- speaking kindly to yourself, even when it's easier to be harsh;
- giving yourself another chance – as many times as you need;
- forgiving yourself – as many times as you need;
- acknowledging that your humanness is not brokenness;
- celebrating yourself as you are while giving yourself the space to change and evolve;
- coming back to yourself and staying there – the world is waiting to see what you can do.

SELF-KINDNESS RITUAL

A QUESTION OF SHOWING UP FOR YOURSELF

Take a moment to reflect on these questions to see
where you are at when it comes to showing up for yourself.

When have you walked out on yourself and paid for it?
Where do you currently need yourself to show up more?
Where do you fear you can't trust yourself?
Which habits are betraying you?
What do you need to give up in order to know
you've got your own back?
When have you shown up for yourself?
What would life be like if you knew you could trust
yourself to do the things that are most important to you?
What would you start, or stop, or do more of, or less of,
if you could trust yourself?

Teach your heart to
hear the whisper of
your intuition.

Once the two are
aligned, anything
is possible.

It felt wrong for too long.
So, she walked away.
And came back
to herself.

Inner peace can come
in the most unexpected
ways, shapes and spaces.

A moment of gratitude
for the patter of rain.

A flash of clarity in the quiet.

The release of worry to trust.

It's there for you to find it
if you dare to look.

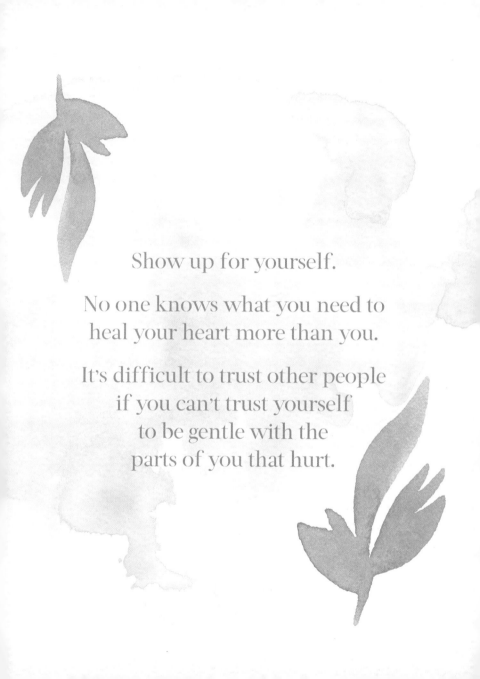

Show up for yourself.

No one knows what you need to
heal your heart more than you.

It's difficult to trust other people
if you can't trust yourself
to be gentle with the
parts of you that hurt.

She's no longer rattled
by what's unresolved.

She simply trusts that
some things pass.

Some things disentangle over time.
Some things were never hers.

And some things will return
when she needs them.

You may have run,
but you came back.

You may have failed,
but you tried again.

You may have fallen,
but you caught yourself.

So, when you doubt if
you can trust yourself,

remember you've already
proven you can.

Your mind will give
you an explanation

for what your heart
already knows.

Your wisdom comes
from listening to both.

Perhaps the beginnings

of personal wisdom are

in trusting that we don't

have to know, do, or be it all,

and we'll still be okay.

Mind: 'I think you should
do it my way.'

Heart: 'You don't listen to
me anyway.'

Soul: 'When you both realise
we're in this together, we'll be
on our way.'

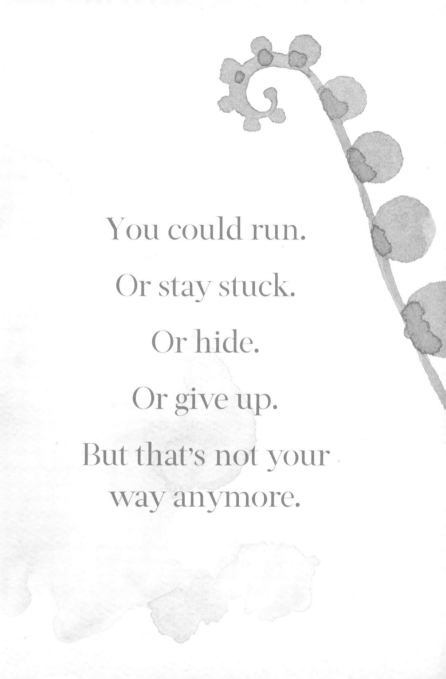

You could run.

Or stay stuck.

Or hide.

Or give up.

But that's not your
way anymore.

Self-Preservation

INWARD KINDNESS FOR OUTWARD KINDNESS

*I*f I had to write this chapter in one word, that word would be *no*. (I don't mean as a response to writing a one-word chapter, although I would also say no to that!). *No* is a two-letter summary of the art of self-preservation: how we buffer ourselves from the demands of life, how we choose to distribute our personal resources and how we manage our relationships with others to avoid becoming depleted. In other words, self-preservation is the art of energy-saving, and the most efficient tool for doing so is saying 'no' when necessary.

No is protection from too much. It's space to simply be. It's the choice to do what you need/want/can. And it's a door that closes on one thing while opening up a 'yes' for another. What you say no to determines the room reserved for the things that matter to you deep down, because when we talk about self-preservation, we're talking about conserving your energy to live in alignment with your values.

We can't give to others if we don't give to ourselves. And to give to ourselves, we need boundaries. No is a boundary. 'I can't right now but I've got time on Thursday,' is a boundary. 'Sundays are for family,' is a boundary. The purpose of a boundary is to protect your personal resources and psychological and physical safety within your self-defined limits. Don't confuse boundaries with brick walls, though

– boundaries are not necessarily for preventing people from becoming close to you or a permanent rejection of an activity or situation. Instead, they are about the lines you draw around yourself based on your current needs for thriving.

But it's not an easy ask for many people who shine with outward kindness. For those for whom giving is akin to breathing, making others happy sits atop the things that give them meaning. While this kind of altruism is admirable, it's not always healthy. I'm not saying don't give, but I am saying that giving beyond what's available in your own tank of reserves is damaging (especially if it's habitual) and will eventually exhaust you. Self-preservation is not selfish. It's exactly the opposite – by taking care of yourself (given no one else can do it for you), you are refuelling your own tanks.

Boundaries often require that we get uncomfortable in the short-term to preserve ourselves in the long-term. Where do you feel someone is taking advantage of you? Where are you feeling disrespected? Where are you feeling resentful towards someone or something but you're continuing to offer yourself up because it's 'just what you have to do'? Doing what's easy (in terms of yours or someone else's comfort) is usually not the road to values alignment. The path of least resistance gets you more of what

'Self-preservation is not selfish. It's exactly the opposite – by taking care of yourself, you are refuelling your own tanks.'

other people need from you without accounting for what you need from yourself. The responsibility for your personal-needs tank and for your giving tank sits with you. One of the laws of being a social creature is that others won't respect you unless you respect yourself first.

Can we talk about death for a moment? I don't mean to turn the conversation morbid, but it's important that we reflect on the ultimate reminder of the preciousness of time, and that's our mortality. Without knowing what the afterlife holds (if there *is* an afterlife), we can generally assume that we get one shot at this earthly existence. If you're struggling with the idea of putting yourself first, let me ask you this: do you want to give away your choices about how you spend your (one) life to someone who's not you?

Say no when you need to. Give yourself permission to rest or to cancel or to opt out or to not do it all. Ask for help when you need to. Put yourself first, so that the best of you is available to give to the people and things that will matter when you're looking back from the end of your days. We get one chance. Don't give away your choices about how you use it.

SELF-KINDNESS RITUAL

RESPECT STARTS WITH YOU

Create restorative space for yourself by:

1. Saying no to things that are costing you too much.

2. Saying yes to things that feed your soul.

3. Asking for help.

4. Taking time out.

5. Creating distance from people who don't or won't respect your boundaries.

6. Planning active self-care (the things that refuel your tanks).

Perhaps it's time to trust
in what you have already
proved to be true:

that you know what you need
better than anyone else.

It's not that she stopped caring.

It's that she's no longer willing to care about the things that need to be forced to work.

In life, there will be people who can't keep up and who are threatened by your growth.

Walk away.

And there will be others who cheer you on and walk beside you through it all.

They are pillars of love and support we must celebrate.

Rushing through life waters
down our experience.

It gives the illusion that we
are getting more out of life,
but in reality, we are just
skimming the surface.

Slow down.

The richest moments are
always the ones that we
bathe in completely.

In a world where so many choices
are demanded of you every day,

don't forget that you have the
choice to choose yourself.

To choose what you need
today to keep going.

To choose to move away
from what's not working.

And to choose where
you're headed next.

Daily choices:

love over hate,

action over anxiety,

vulnerability over shame,

authenticity over masks,

calm over chaos,

intuition over expectations,

response over reaction,

awareness over fear.

After too many lessons of
exhausting her reserves

(for worthwhile reasons and
those not so much),

she finally learned that she
could ask of herself *only*
the equivalent of what she
was giving herself.

And she learned to check
her reasons.

She said no

because she only

has so many

yeses to give,

and they are reserved

for the things that

propel her heart.

'Busy' is not an identity.
It's a lifestyle, and a
dangerous one at that.
Your worth is not
dependent on your
calendar, but your
inner peace is.
Make space for it.

Daily choices:

presence over hustle,

community over competition,

flow over force,

compassion over judgement,

acceptance over struggle,

progress over perfection,

brave over stuck.

Self-Discovery

THE ENDLESS JOURNEY

*W*elcome to the last pages of our exploration of self-kindness, lovely one. I want to leave you with a keen awareness of your potential when you befriend yourself, which is why I've chosen to paint self-discovery as the final brushstroke on our canvas. Being kind to yourself in each of the practices we have reflected upon isn't a neat 30-day program. It's a lifelong commitment. We don't ever *arrive*, we continue to discover ourselves along the way and forever hold the responsibility to take care of ourselves as we unfold.

With the privilege of age comes a sense of learning about yourself. If you allow them, the seasons of change and growth will unwrap your layers, so you may know yourself a little more with every experience. By staying open and willing, curious and gentle with yourself, living becomes a conscious process of gathering wisdom about your authentic nature. This wisdom feeds the roots of your self-acceptance. It helps you offer yourself forgiveness, and it reminds you that you can trust yourself.

While there are no hard and fast instructions for learning about yourself (please don't get caught up in the 'right way' to do it because there isn't one), you can help the process along by paying attention. Pay attention to what hurts you, what nourishes you, what ignites you, what frustrates you, what relaxes you, what makes you uneasy, what you wouldn't do again but couldn't have learned another way. Pay attention to it all and, as you do, give yourself room to move, try it on and figure out what fits. Your growth is a gift – don't criticise, humiliate or otherwise dishonour yourself through the process. And for what it's worth, here are a few notes for your pockets on your journey.

1. If you buy into society's standards or rules about what makes someone enough, you'll always consider yourself to be lacking.

2. Your boundaries are your responsibility. You're allowed to place them where they fit for you, enforce them as you need to and adjust them as you learn more about yourself.

3. Devote time to reflecting on what you're doing well, what you've done well and what you'll do well in the future. More time than you spend thinking about your mistakes.

4. Your relationship with yourself is more important than your relationship with anyone else (including your partner and your children) because it defines every other relationship in your life.

5. The people who love you depend on you to love yourself, so that your love for each other can be free.

6. What you say no to determines what you have room to say yes to.

7. When you speak about yourself, remember that you are listening. When you speak to yourself, remember that you are listening. Always.

8. Forgiveness is freedom. The more forgiveness you offer yourself, the freer your experience of life will be.

9. The more forgiving you are with yourself, the more generous you will be in your relationships with others.

10. You will stuff up. We all do. You are human. You are okay.

11. Don't apply hindsight to your younger self. It's entirely unfair to punish yourself for what you didn't know then.

12. The criticisms you've received in the past can very easily become a believable collective voice that condemns you, without realising that you're being driven by a faceless captor with no control over you.

13. The signs of ageing on your face and your skin are markers of the privilege of continuing life. Be grateful to yourself for still being here. You've made it this far!

SELF-KINDNESS RITUAL

WHAT I NOW KNOW

In this powerful reflection exercise, take yourself
somewhere that inspires your heart. Somewhere you can
think with clarity. Somewhere you feel peaceful. Take a
pen and your favourite notebook with you and, in 10–15
minutes, write down all the lessons you can think of
that you have learned about yourself so far. Pay special
attention to the areas in which you have grown, expanded,
gone deeper and become more authentic. Note the ways
in which you've accepted yourself. Highlight the things
you have come to love about yourself. Make space for the
things you forgive yourself for. You can use any format you
like – the important thing is that you do this exercise with
unconditional positive regard for yourself.

_____

_____

_____

_____

_____

_____

_____

_____

Mind:
'I think we're doing okay here.'

Heart:
'Just okay? I'm as open as
I've ever been!'

Soul:
'It's called alignment,
my friends. Welcome.'

Changing your mind
is not weakness.

It's a response to gathering
wisdom – about yourself,
another or the world – that
widens your view beyond
where you could
previously see.

You have the choice
to choose again.

She was only able to
map out her true path
by first going down
a road that wasn't
meant for her.

She realised she
didn't have to go
and find herself.

When she peeled back
the layers of everyone
else's expectations,
she found that she'd
been there all along.

Through the healing she had
a flash of recognition.

Underneath the layers of hurt
and fear and doubt,

she felt familiar.

Finally, her soul reminded
her of herself.

She'd been there all along.

There's magic in the rumblings
of a shift about to take place.

It's here that you get glimpses of
the next version of yourself.

The one that has cast off what
no longer works and is peeking
out to confirm the world is
ready for her.

Let her out!

Change may be the quiet,
slow stretch of life that
happens until it's out of shape
and doesn't fit anymore.

Or it may be the quake and shatter
of a moment turning inside out.

Or somewhere in between.

Grieve for it.

Heal with it.

Rise upon it.

Wear it anew.

Sometimes we choose change.

Sometimes change chooses us.

Whichever your experience is right now,

what matters is your belief in your own strength and spirit.

She's got a revolution

happening within.

She's seen too much magic
in the unexpected detours
to cling to 'how it should be'.

For her, off track means growth
is just around the corner.

All she has to do is get out
of her own way.

Kindly
and
gently,
forward

And so, we move forward, kindly and gently.

Holding our own hand.

Being a friend to ourselves.

Doing the work for ourselves, with ourselves.

We rise out of the ashes and blaze a trail
in our own way.

Without apology for feeling, for needing,
for creating, for loving.

Without apology for being true to ourselves.

We make space for growth.

Committed always to our own version
of courageous living.

And we completely accept ourselves:
every atom that is our being.

We are human. We are whole.
And we honour ourselves for it.

A FEW WORDS OF GRATITUDE

As always, my deepest thanks sit first and foremost with my people: the ones who have bestowed upon me kindness after kindness in receiving my words with willing hearts and open minds. You are my fellow brave beings, and the gift of you reminding me to love myself through your own journeys into self-kindness has transformed me. Your kindness inspires me every day.

For always being kinder to me than I am to myself and for loving me on every step of the journey, I will never have words valuable enough to express my gratitude for my wife, Nyssa. My gratitude for you is spiritual.

Thank you to Bennett for being the most profound teacher in the art of self-kindness. You've brought me back to myself.

To my mum and dad – for giving me more than I could have ever asked for. I can only hope that you know how deeply grateful I am to love and be loved by such generous beings. To my brother Nick – thank you for making me the proudest sister there ever was (and, also, for not getting eaten by a shark when you crossed Bass Strait on a stand-up paddleboard).

To my mum and dad-in-law – you two are the Masters of Kindness. Thank you for setting the bar so high – hearts like yours are rare and I am so bloody lucky that my second family is you.

To Bec, Jen, Em and Erin – thank you for being my saviours, protectors and cheerleaders, and always getting me, even when I don't get myself.

Thank you to my agent, Clare, and to my publishing team at Pan Macmillan: Ingrid, Virginia and Alissa. Thank you for making art out of my words and for being so kind and encouraging during the creative process.

I am myself because of each of you. Thank you.

First published 2019 in Macmillan
by Pan Macmillan Australia Pty Limited
1 Market Street, Sydney, New South Wales
Australia 2000

A CIP catalogue record for this book is available from the National Library
of Australia: http://catalogue.nla.gov.au

Design by Alissa Dinallo
Colour + reproduction by Splitting Image Colour Studio
Printed in China by Imago

We advise that the information contained in this book does not negate
personal responsibility on the part of the reader for their own health and safety.
It is recommended that individually tailored advice is sought from your healthcare
or medical professional. The publishers and their respective employees, agents
and authors are not liable for injuries or damage occasioned to any person as
a result of reading or following the information contained in this book.

10 9 8 7 6 5 4 3 2 1